These three essays by an [...] recognized authority on [...] Central and Eastern Euro[pe...] thoughtful summary of long years of scholarship and first-hand knowledge.

The title is taken from a phrase, familiar to the author in his youth, which designated Germany as the heart of Europe and explained Europe's tragedies in the twentieth century as due to the fact that its heart was sick. Seton-Watson views this "sick heart" as comprising not only Germany itself, but also the wider region influenced by German culture, particularly the lands where German-speaking populations overlap with peoples of other languages.

T[...] essay examines the sickness of the L[...] lands, beginning with the co[...] the "Old Empires"—the Hab[sburg] onarchy and the German and Russ[ian empi]res—which brought about the creati[on of ne]w or enlarged small states. The sec[ond essa]y is a discussion of this brief period o[f nationa]l freedom, pointing out factors tha[t brough]t it to an end. The last essay deals [with th]e period after the Second World War when most of these states fell under the power of a new empire, the Soviet Union. The author argues that the Soviet Union, by trying to destroy the national identities of the eighty million Europeans under its jurisdiction, is keeping all Europe in a latently explosive condition.

[...] history at the University of London. Among the books he has written are *Eastern Europe between the Wars, 1918–1941*; *The East European Revolution*; and *Neither War nor Peace*.

THE "SICK HEART" OF MODERN EUROPE

The "Sick Heart"
of Modern Europe

The Problem of the Danubian Lands

BY HUGH SETON-WATSON

University of Washington Press
Seattle and London

Copyright © 1975 by the University of Washington Press
Printed in the United States of America

Library of Congress Cataloging in Publication Data

Seton-Watson, Hugh.
    The "sick heart" of modern Europe.

    "Three Walker-Ames lectures given at the University of
Washington."
    1. Central Europe—Politics and government—Addresses, es-
says, lectures. 2. Europe, Eastern—Politics and government—
Addresses, essays, lectures. 3. Minorities—Central Europe—
Addresses, essays, lectures. 4. Minorities—Europe, Eastern—
Addresses, essays, lectures. I. Title.
DR38.2.S47   320.9'43   74-30170
ISBN 0-295-95360-8

Foreword

This slender volume contains the texts of three lectures delivered at the University of Washington in the fall of 1973 by Hugh Seton-Watson, professor of history at the School of Slavonic and East European Studies of the University of London. At that time, Professor Seton-Watson was visiting the University of Washington as a Walker-Ames professor teaching a course for the Russian and East European Area Studies Program of the Institute for Comparative and Foreign Area Studies.

The Walker-Ames professorships were established by Mr. Edwin Gardner Ames (d. 1935) and his wife Mrs. Maud Walker-Ames (d. 1931) "to guarantee to the State of Washington the scholarly and educational services of the most distinguished minds available in this and other countries." The list of those who have held this title since 1936 includes the names of numerous men of great distinction from many countries. They represent a wide variety of academic disciplines and professions: professors, lawyers, actors, poets, industrial designers, musicians, painters, and scientists. In conformity with the wishes of Mr. and Mrs. Ames, the holders of the professorship were selected purely on the grounds of their achievements, irrespective of the disciplines and professions in which they excelled or of their homelands or affiliations. They have indeed brought to the university and the state of Washington many benefits. Students have profited from their presence in the classrooms, the faculty has been given the opportunity to exchange ideas with them, and the general public has been enriched by their lectures. The Walker-Ames Lectures represent intellectual highlights of the academic year at the University of Washington.

The presence of Professor Seton-Watson on campus was a case in point. This world-famous historian, and Fellow of the British Academy, was born on 15 February 1916, the son of Professor R. W. Seton-Watson, who was an influential publicist, eminent historian, and adviser to statesmen of several countries. After attending Winchester, Hugh Seton-Watson enrolled at New College at Oxford where he studied for the degree of Philosophy, Politics and Economics. During 1940–41 he was attached to the British Legation in Romania, and subsequently served, from 1941 to 1944, with the Special Forces General Headquarters for the Middle East. In 1946 he was appointed Fellow and Praelector at University College, Oxford, and was promoted to his present position in London in 1951. Professor Seton-Watson has visited the United States on numerous occasions to attend conferences and to lecture. He was visiting professor at Columbia University in 1957–58 and at Indiana University in 1973. He was also Fellow at the Center of Advanced Studies in the Behavioral Sciences at Stanford University in 1963–64.

Sons of distinguished fathers seldom attain similar rank in the same profession. An exception to this rule, Hugh Seton-Watson, like his father before him, has gained international recognition as an authority on the history of Eastern Europe. That area is usually defined as the segment of the continent lying between the German- and Russian-speaking parts of Europe. Its complexity is so great that most scholars who devote their attention to it exclude not only Germany and Russia, but also often leave aside the Baltic States and the Ukraine. In his definition of Eastern Europe, Professor Seton-Watson includes the often neglected regions and has made himself also an expert in the history of those German-speaking parts of Europe (Austria and the German Democratic Republic) whose history is closely interwoven with that of the peoples usually studied by East European specialists. Moreover, he has become equally well known as a historian of Russia/Soviet Union.

Professor Seton-Watson's unusually broad interest is anything but academic. He has traveled widely through these lands and his extraordinary talent and love for languages has made it possible for him to converse in their native languages with those whom he meets. Widely read not only in the history but also in the literature of the various people, he brings an unmatched understanding and empathy to his scholarship.

A prolific writer, Seton-Watson has produced a staggering number of articles published in the most influential journals at home and abroad. His many books testify further to his broad interests and constitute major contributions to scholarship. They include *East-*

ern Europe between the Wars; *The East European Revolution; The Pattern of Communist Revolution*, simultaneously published as *From Lenin to Malenkov*, and later republished as *From Lenin to Khrushchev; The Decline of Imperial Russia; Neither War nor Peace; The New Imperialism; Nationalism and Communism: Essays, 1946–1963*; and *The Russian Empire, 1801–1917*. These books have become essential reading for historians of Russia/U.S.S.R. and East European countries. They have been widely used as texts and reference works in universities and read generally throughout the English-speaking world.

In his three Walker-Ames lectures, Professor Seton-Watson presents a succinct and remarkably clear explanation of how and why the peoples of these varied East European countries have arrived at their present position in today's world. Their problems have been and are more than local or national; they are European and in many respects worldwide in their implications and involvement. Seton-Watson, out of his detailed knowledge, defines the intricate issues for specialists and nonspecialists alike. He thereby opens the door to the history of this crucial region for students who approach it for the first time. At the same time he offers new and original interpretations which will stimulate specialists to rethink what has previously been generally accepted.

Particularly notable is the spirit and objectivity of his discussion. He picks no favorites nor renders arbitrary judgments. Instead, he seeks to understand and sympathize. Professor Seton-Watson can think like a Czech, feel like a Romanian, speak like a Pole, laugh like a Hungarian, weep like a Serb, and at the same time remain an objective, scholarly outsider. This deep understanding and *Mitgefühl* coupled with a rigorous, self-critical scholarship give Professor Seton-Watson's evaluation of recent East European history its special flavor and value.

PETER F. SUGAR
Professor of History,
Associate Director, Institute for
Comparative and Foreign Area Studies;
Director of the Russian and East
European Area Studies Program,
University of Washington

Contents

THE "SICK HEART" OF MODERN EUROPE

The Old Empires

My title is taken from a phrase which became familiar to me in my younger days—whether from my father, who was much concerned with these problems, or from my schoolteachers, or from my first experience of travel by myself abroad, I do not remember. The phrase was that Germany was the heart of Europe, and that all the troubles of the last few generations in Europe had derived from the fact that the heart was sick. As I traveled and studied more, it seemed to me that the heart was not so much Germany as the wider region deeply influenced by German culture, especially the lands where German-speaking populations overlap with peoples of other languages. One could make a good case for a much smaller heart; Bohemia—where Germans and Czechs meet, the very center of the continent, the land of which Bismarck is said to have declared that who holds it, holds Central Europe. And certainly Bohemia has been sick through most of this century, and appears almost mortally sick today. But I prefer to think of the heart as all the lands through which the Danube flows, from Germany to Romania.

It may be suggested that nobody can have a heart that is about a third of its total size. This is true, and of course my title is a bad one. However, titles in the humanities do not, I suggest, always need to serve the same purpose as titles in the natural sciences. In the latter they ought, no doubt, to be labels precisely describing the contents; in the former they are often only intended to guide one's thoughts in a general direction. This I hope my title may do.

My emphasis will be on the non-German rather than the German regions, but I should say at the outset that Germans and German culture have been inextricably mixed up in this region, in a way that is certainly not true of French, or Russian, or English, or Italian, or American. Somewhere in this region lies the heart, but I at least cannot pinpoint it, for each part merges imperceptibly into the next.

I propose to keep to a minimum my mention of individual people and places. I shall also be concentrating on interpretation rather than facts — though the facts cannot all be left out. Let me also say that the interpretation is my own, and that it is very fallible. The story, if I may change my metaphors, has three acts, and cannot be understood without following all three. The first act encompasses the first eighteen years of the century; the second goes from the end of the First to the end of the Second World War; the third covers the last decades.

At the beginning of this century, the Danube flowed through the German Empire, the Habsburg Monarchy, the independent states of Serbia and Romania, the Ottoman Empire (which still held nominal sovereignty

4

over Bulgaria), and the Russian Empire (which held part of the river's huge delta).

Admiration for the splendid culture of Austria-Hungary, and regret for its destruction, have become a cliché among historians, journalists, and politicians. I am willing to go along some of the way with the mourners. Among those who regretted its fall, be it said in passing, was my father, who has been called, not without reason, one of the monarchy's grave-diggers. But I do not think the regret should be confined to Austria-Hungary. Let us not forget the glories of the German Empire, which lay perhaps more in science and industry than in arts and letters—where Austria was, in its last decades, more productive. Let us also not forget the glories of the Russian Empire—considerable in the sciences, but brilliant in the poetry of the silver age and in the flowering of the visual arts and drama. All three empires, it may be argued, were replaced by barbarism (save for the brief intervals of Weimar culture and Masaryk's republic). This is certainly a defensible argument, though there is another side to the problem, as we shall see later. Meanwhile, however, by all means let us pay homage to the three empires and regret their fall, yet at the same time recognize that all three were destroyed by forces which to some extent they had called into being and were unable to master, by human needs which they had failed to satisfy or even to recognize.

All three empires suffered from severe social and political discontents. In both Austria-Hungary and European Russia, up to the end of the First World War, the great majority of the population were peasants. The agricultural societies of both monarchies were bedeviled by problems of technical backwardness, maldistribution of land, unjust and counterproductive taxation, and relative overpopulation, which it is not possible to examine in this brief survey. The German Empire was not free from such problems, especially in the eastern parts of Prussia where noble estates predominated and German and Polish peasants coexisted. The most important social stresses in the German Empire were, however, in the industrial field; Germany demonstrated both the achievements and the abuses of large-scale capitalism. The industrial class struggle, prominent in Germany, had also made its appearance in both Austria and Russia. In all three empires also, the struggle between absolutism and democracy had been passing through successive stages from unbending autocracy to conservative monarchy on the one side, and from liberal constitutionalism to socialism on the other. This struggle had come to the fore in 1848, and it was in vigorous progress when Europe was plunged into war in 1914.

Social, political, and constitutional struggles form the background for what will be discussed, but the essence of my theme is nationalism. All sorts of social and political aspirations became fused, in a variety of compounds, in the national movements in the Danube lands. It is extremely hard to unscramble these constituent elements, and within my present limits of space it is quite impossible. It was necessary to draw attention, at the outset, to the existence of the background. I shall now attack by main theme, and shall concern myself at first almost solely with Austria-Hungary.

The basis of legitimacy of the Habsburg Monarchy in the first half of the nineteenth century had been *Kaisertreue*, devotion to the emperor. If his subjects were loyal to him, in that station in life to which they were called (peasants, tradesmen, officials or noble-men), they enjoyed the sovereign's protection, regardless of the province in which they lived or the language which they spoke. In earlier times there had not been equal treatment of religious belief, but in the 1780s, Emperor Joseph II had introduced religious tolerance. He had also encouraged education, which at the lowest level was to be given in the vernacular language. The growth of schools had created new cultural elites among the more backward peoples, and had caused the ideas of the European Enlightenment to spread among them. From this process had emerged both liberal and nationalist demands—demands for constitutional government, and for organized self-government, for different language-groups, which now began to regard themselves as nations. Both sets of demands had been rejected for decades on end by Metternich, but he had been overthrown by the revolutions of 1848. The revolutions were crushed, but the subsequent attempt at more or less enlightened absolutism broke down when Austria lost two wars within a decade. Emperor Francis Joseph was obliged to make a compromise in 1867 with the leaders of the Hungarian nationalist movement, and the so-called period of Dualism was introduced: Austria became Austria-Hungary.

The essence of Dualism was that a different basis of legitimacy was adopted in two parts of the monarchy. In the east and south (in the Kingdom of Hungary) sovereignty was claimed for the Hungarian nation. In the west and north (which I shall call Austria for simplicity's sake, though that is not a strictly correct description) the basis of legitimacy remained as previously, *Kaisertreue.* Let us consider the operation of these principles in each.

Hungary after 1867 was regarded by its rulers as a "national state." There was one "political nation": the Hungarian (or Magyar). There were also numerous communities which were described as "nationalities," a category at a lower level than a nation. This word (in the Magyar language *nemzetiség*) was taken from the German *Nationalität,* which does not mean the same thing as the English word "nationality," whether in its Britannic or its American usage. It was adopted in Austria to denote the various distinct cultural communities which the authorities knew to exist within the monarchy, but for which they refused to use the word "nation." In Austria there were, in the official view, no nations, not even an Austrian nation. In Hungary, by contrast, there was one Magyar nation. Membership in this nation had been limited, in past centuries, to the nobility, a precise, legally defined social group. Non-members of this nation were relegated to the *misera contribuens plebs,* the miserable tax-paying mob. In 1848 the revolutionary Hungarian government abolished the privileges of the nobility, and admitted all classes to the nation. A new condition was however imposed: members of the Hungarian nation should speak the Magyar language and regard themselves as

Magyars. If they did this, they were of course entitled to go on using their own languages (Slovak, Romanian, Serbo-Croatian, German, or a dialect of Ukrainian) in their homes and in their private lives, but their public language must be Magyar: their private language did not confer on them the status of nation. There was to be no Slovak, Romanian, or other nation in Hungary, only one Magyar nation. In 1868 a Nationality Law was passed, which protected the cultural rights of the non-Magyars (I shall use this cumbrous word in preference to the ambiguous and tendentious word "nationalities"), while insisting on the supremacy of the single Magyar "political nation." However, in the subsequent decades this law was in practice more and more ignored; many of the privately-financed schools in which instruction was given to peasant children in non-Magyar languages were suppressed; education laws introduced more and more rigid regulations about teaching *of* the Magyar language and *in* the Magyar language; a whole system of legalistic trickery was devised, by which newspapers in non-Magyar languages could be bankrupted by fines, or suppressed outright; excuses were found for sending non-Magyar political leaders to prison for a year or so at a time; and there were occasional violent clashes in which non-Magyar crowds were fired on by Hungarian gendarmes. All this added up to nasty petty persecution rather than really cruel oppression, as judged by later twentieth century standards. Still, it caused enormous resentment among the non-Magyars, indignation among their foreign friends, and produced ever stronger and more bitter anti-Magyar nationalist activity within Hungary by Slovaks, Romanians, Serbs, and the rest, who insisted that they were not just second-rate *nationalities* but fully formed *nations* entitled to equal status with the Magyar nation.

It is only fair to adduce certain arguments in justification, or at least in palliation, of the authors of this *Magyarization* policy. The Magyar leaders were former liberals or radicals, who accepted the belief, then widespread among European liberals and especially in France, that government must be centralized, and that local diversities and autonomies were a reactionary obstacle to progress. The Magyar leaders believed that, by inducing the non-Magyars to give up their Slovak or Romanian speech and to adopt Magyar, they were opening to them access to a much higher culture. In short, they were doing the non-Magyars a kind service and were acting as philanthropists. The Magyar leaders were also genuinely afraid of dangers threatening them from the neighboring small states. The Romanian-speaking subjects of Hungary lived right along the mountain border of the kingdom of Romania, from which a propaganda campaign was being launched for the union of all Romanians within one state. The only way the Magyar leaders saw to save their Romanian-speaking subjects from being infected with the virus of what was known as Daco-Romanism, was to force them to become Magyars. Similar considerations applied to the Serbian subjects of Hungary who lived along the border with the Kingdom of Serbia. As for the Slovaks, they had, it is true, no foreign neighbors dangerous to Hungary, but both they and the Czechs, who lived to the west of them—inside the monarchy but in territory ruled not from Budapest but from Vienna—were much addicted to Panslav rhetoric, resounding phrases about solidarity with the great Slav brothers the Russians. Not only was Russia the most important potential enemy of the monarchy, but the Magyars had every reason to loathe Russians, since it had been Russian troops which had suppressed the Hungarian Revolution in 1849. So the Slovaks too had to be made harmless by being turned into Magyars. But though one can understand why the Magyar leaders felt like this, one must say that their policy was counterproductive: they did not make Magyars, they only made enemies. The dangers of Daco-Romanism and Panslavism were quite small in the 1870s, but Magyarization increased them. The dire warnings of the early Magyarizers proved to be self-fulfilling prophecies.

It is true that at first Magyarization appeared to be succeeding. The cities became centers of Magyar culture. After 1867, rapidly developing industry and trade drew many peasants from the non-Magyar villages, who then became Magyars. A prominent part was played in this process by the Jews, who were very prominent in business life, well treated by the Hungarian government, and who became enthusiastic Magyars —and even Magyarizers. However, the tide began to turn early in the century. Non-Magyars who had passed through Magyar schools increasingly used their talents to lead their own peoples against the Magyar political and social system. Trained lawyers or doctors of Slovak birth insisted on remaining Slovaks and on fighting for the Slovak national cause. In the Hungarian cities centers of Magyar culture and countercenters of non-Magyar culture existed side by side. For example, Kassa (Košice or Kaschau) was both a Magyar and a Slovak center; Kolozsvár (Cluj or Klausenburg), a Magyar and a Romanian; and Ujvidék (Novi Sad or Neusatz), a Magyar and a Serbian. There were also ancient centers of urban German culture in Transylvania, such as Kronstadt (Brássó or Braşov) or Hermannstadt (Sibiu or Nagyszeben).

It is also true that there was a common interest between many Magyars and non-Magyars. The liberalism of the Hungarian rulers, with their heroic 1848 past, was of a strictly limited kind. They included landed gentry, great landowners, and increasingly, professional bureaucrats. All three categories distrusted the peasant majority, and kept them out of political life by restricted voting rights. By contrast, the demand for universal suffrage was common to Magyars and non-Magyars. This was most clearly understood by the Social Democrats. However, the appeal of the Social Democats was almost entirely limited to Budapest, the great industrial center of the kingdom, and depended very heavily on the support of the Magyar working class. There were a few non-Magyar socialist leaders, but it cannot be said that they had much influence on their own peoples. Some nonsocialist, non-Magyar leaders nevertheless understood the need for alliance with the Magyar people against the Magyar rulers. For example, the Slovak agrarian Milan Hodža addressed electoral meetings in central Hungary, explaining in excellent Magyar to Magyar peasants the grievances of Slovak peasants, and appealing for solidarity. There were also friendships between Magyar and non-Magyar intellectuals: that between the great Hungarian poet Endre Ady and the great Romanian poet Octavian Goga comes to mind. Lastly I must mention Oszkár Jászi, the Magyar sociologist, who had a vision of a higher Magyar culture, absorbing into itself all the cultures of the various peoples, as American culture was—so he believed—absorbing the cultures of the immigrant peoples into a higher American culture. Unfortunately, none of these bridge builders was listened to, and Hungary was not reformed, but dissolved. Some of these men stopped trying to build bridges; Hodža remained a good democrat, but was increasingly conservative and nationalistic, while Goga became a Romanian fascist. Ady died young and in poverty in 1919, and Jászi died in 1957 in the United States, full of honors, but still rejected by his own country's rulers.

In Austria the principle of *Kaisertreue*, the notion of loyalty to an overarching dynasty raised above linguistic, religious, or national divisions, remained official doctrine until the end. No single "nationality" was to be entitled to privileges at the expense of others. As far as the conscious policy of the rulers were concerned, it also remained a practical reality, with the important exception of one outlying province, Galicia. Here the far-reaching self-government, which was granted by the Vienna government in the late 1860s, enabled the Polish half of the population to rule at the expense of the Ukrainian half, though it is true that some attempt was made from Vienna to safeguard Ukrainian rights; and that after universal suffrage was

13

introduced in Austria in 1907, and the Ukrainian peasants could send their representatives to the Vienna parliament (*Reichsrat*) the power of the Polish rulers was severely limited.

However, we must look not only at political intentions and institutions, but also at economic and cultural realities. Seen from these points of view, there can be no doubt of the predominance of the German element in the Austrian half of the monarchy. This is the element of truth in the cliché, found in most textbooks of European history up to 1914, that Austria-Hungary was based on a German-Magyar condominium over the other peoples. In the strictly political sphere, this cliché is not true.

The German-speaking people of the monarchy were economically more advanced, socially more complex, and enjoyed a higher level of culture, than the others. They were followed at a rapidly diminishing interval by the Czechs (in Bohemia and Moravia) and the Slovenes (in the Alpine provinces of Styria, Carniola, Carinthia, and Gorizia), who were developing very fast but had the disadvantage that their languages were not known outside their homelands, and that they therefore had to use German in order to participate in European culture. In the economic and cultural development of the German-speaking lands of Austria, Jews had played an extremely important part. Great numbers of Jews had gladly accepted assimilation, and were proud to belong to the German cultural world. The predominant outlook among the educated elite of German-speaking subjects of the monarchy in the later decades of the nineteenth century was a mixture of conservative and

liberal thought; devotion to the monarchy was com-
bined with belief in industrial growth, urbanization,
education, and free exchange of ideas. This outlook
was, on the whole, common to German-speaking Austrians of Christian, Judaic, or no religion, to bureaucrats
and members of the free professions and noblemen.
They would think of themselves in a sense as Germans
as well as Austrians. They felt themselves to belong to a
single German culture, which embraced the people of
the German Empire; but their political loyalty was
given to the Austrian dynasty. They did not feel that
they belonged to a single German nation, destined to
dominate other nations.

There was however a strong minority to whom this
attitude was not enough. These were the German nationalists, who bitterly regretted the failure of the
Greater German (*grossdeutsch*) programme of 1848,
which had aimed at uniting all Germans in one state.
They hated the Habsburgs as enemies of the German
nation. These German nationalists were strongest in
the regions where populations of German and of other
speech overlapped—in the Bohemian and Alpine borderlands. Their enemies were the Czechs, the Slovenes,
and to a somewhat lesser extent, the Italians. As the
Bohemian borderlands for the most part joined the
frontier with the German Empire, the idea of secession
from Austria and of unification with Germany was especially strong among them (though it was certainly
always a minority viewpoint as long as the monarchy
lasted). German nationalists were also extremely hostile
to Jews. Jewish liberalism, which slurred over the dis-
tinctions between the Reich and the monarchy, be-

tween the German *nation* and the naturally inferior Slav *nationalities,* was their main enemy.

The case of Bohemia deserves a little more attention. In the Middle Ages the kingdom of Bohemia held a glorious place in Europe, and in the Hussite wars the embattled land had withstood the armies and crusaders drawn from all Catholic Europe. In the fifteenth and sixteenth centuries a Bohemian nation began to emerge. However, this nation cannot be simply identified as those who spoke Czech; there were Czech-speakers and German-speakers on both sides in the Hussite wars. This Bohemian nation was destroyed after the disaster of 1620—the Battle of the White Mountain when the rebellious Bohemian nobility were defeated by the imperial army, and the series of murderous campaigns known as the Thirty Years War was let loose. In these wars the old nobility was destroyed by execution, exile, and confiscation, and its lands were given to new men. The population of this once rich land was reduced by more than one third, and the Czech-speakers were reduced to a peasantry excluded from political life.

The Josephine reforms brought a cultural revival, following the earlier recovery of the economy and an increase in the population. From the Czech-speaking masses, new cultural elites emerged who adopted the ideas of the European Enlightenment, and who identified the cause they were to serve with the Czech-speaking population. At the same time similar processes took place among the German-speaking population. Thus, instead of the revival of the old Bohemian nation, there appeared in Bohemia two nations—a Czech nation and a German nation. The nobility for a time stood above the conflict between these two, and pursued the ideal of a more autonomous Bohemia based on its provincial identity. However, both German and Czech nationalism began to affect part of the nobility.

At the beginning of the twentieth century both the Bohemian Germans and the Czechs had maximum and minimum demands. The German maximum demand was an all-German Bohemia, with the Czechs in a definitely subordinate position. Their minimum demand was that Bohemia should be divided on the basis of language, with the regions of predominant German and predominant Czech speech as completely separated political units; some German nationalists would have liked to incorporate the separate German Bohemia in the German Reich. The maximum demand of the Czech nationalists was an all-Czech Bohemia, with the Germans in a definitely subordinate position. Their minimum demand was the maintenance of a single Bohemia (respecting the sanctity of the historical frontiers of Bohemia) with equal rights for both languages. None of these demands were compatible with each other. Even the minimum demands meant an intolerable predominance of one over the other. If Bohemia were divided, all the industrial regions would have gone to the German unit, and the strategic frontiers would have disappeared, thus placing the Czech unit at the mercy of the German unit—which would have been expected to have the German Reich not only physically, but also politically behind it. If the two languages had equal status within a united Bohemia, sooner or later the Germans feared that the Czechs, outnumbering them two to one and possessing a higher natural increase rate, would impose Czech language and culture on them. Faced with these incompatible positions, the Vienna governments made many well-meant but halfhearted attempts to reconcile the two bitter nations, but all attempts were defeated by the extremists of one or the other camp.

It is perhaps convenient, even at this stage, to anticipate events which more properly belong to later periods of my story, and to note that during the twentieth century both maximum and both minimum demands were achieved for a time. The Czech minimum was achieved during the twenty years of the First Czechoslovak Republic. But it did not satisfy most Germans, and the more extreme German nationlists asserted that in fact it was the Czech maximum that was implemented—that is, an all-Czech Bohemia. The minimum German program was achieved at the Munich settlement of 1938, and lasted five months. While it lasted, it placed the Czechs at the mercy of Germany, as Czech opponents of the German minimum demands had said it would since the 1890s. The German maximum demand was put into effect in March 1939 by Hitler, and lasted for six years. Finally, the Czech maximum program was achieved in 1945, was fully implemented, has been in force for twenty-eight years, and indeed appears at present to be irreversible. Two brief points might be made. The first is that of all four attempts the last undoubtedly caused the largest total volume of human suffering. The second is that this last attempt has only been achieved at the cost of enslaving the whole Czech nation to another imperial power incomparably more ruthless than the Habsburg.

Let us return to the Habsburg Monarchy. What were the forces which supported the monarchy in the face of so much disruptive nationalism? They were five: the officer corps, the civil bureaucracy, the Catholic hierarchy (though not always the lower levels of the Church), the Jews, and the Social Democrats. The last two perhaps deserve a few words of explanation. The support of German-speaking Jews for Austria was rather different from the support of Magyar-speaking Jews for Hungary. Austrian Jews and Hungarian Jews alike spoke the language of liberalism: the two great newspapers *Neue Freie Presse* in Vienna and *Pester Lloyd* in Budapest, both owned and written by Jews, formed an alliance—their critics would say an unholy alliance—which gave expression to the mythical (that is, part real, part fictitious) condominium of Germans and Magyars which has already been referred to. Yet the two forces were different. The Austrian Jews were above all *kaisertreu* and genuinely tried to stand above nationalist passions; the Hungarian Jews were Magyar nationalists. As for the Social Democrats, they were of course in principle republicans, not to say revolutionaries. They can hardly be described as explicitly *kaisertreu*; yet implicitly they regarded the warring nationalisms as greater enemies than the emperor. It was more important to them to preserve the territorial unity of the empire than to overthrow the dynasty. This is a not unfair comment on the published works and political activities of Karl Renner and Otto Bauer.

Arrayed against these forces were the various nationalisms, from the strong and militant Magyars to the

19

hesitant and still near-*kaisertreu* Slovenes. But there was also another force, less obvious at the time, yet which today we can see as the most destructive of all. This was a kind of German political nationalism, moderate yet dynamic, which was steadily increasing among the German-speaking population of the monarchy. The German-Austrian Alliance, made in 1879 by Bismarck and Andrássy, was a conventional diplomatic instrument, an agreement between two sovereigns for their mutual advantage, with no ideological undertones. But thirty years later it had changed its nature. There was a widespread feeling that the German Reich was not just an ally, but a second fatherland, that there was a common cause of *Deutschtum* (Germanity), which both empires were defending. This feeling was even beginning to affect army officers and bureaucrats. Its most characteristic exponent was the Christian Social Party of Dr. Karl Lueger, which played at German nationalism and anti-Semitic demagogy without being really serious about either, but which made a substantial and lasting contribution to the poisoning of the political atmosphere of Vienna. The *Grossösterreich* advocated by some Christian Socials was much the same as the Greater Germany dreamed up by the Pangerman League in the German Reich. Even Jews were affected by the new German political nationalism, without ceasing to be liberals; and even some socialists were affected without ceasing altogether to be socialists. All these elements were still *kaisertreu*. There was no question for them of seceding from the monarchy to join Germany; the German nationalist parties which did wish to secede, remained always a minority among

German-speaking Austrian subjects. There was even a good deal of dislike for the Prussians cultivated in the army, reflected in the extraordinary lack of coordination between the plans of the two General Staffs. Yet the growing German nationalism, coupled with a growing belief that Germans as a superior nation were entitled to rule over inferior Slavs and Latins, was an undeniable, though retrospectively unquantifiable, feature of the last years of the Habsburg monarchy.

This trend was sensed, feared, resented, and exaggerated by the non-Germans. This was curiously least true of the Magyars—at least of their political class—though the Magyars had a longer tradition of suspicion and dislike toward Germans than any other Danubian nation. Essentially, the reason for this is that the Magyar rulers believed a place was to be assured to them as partners in the new Europe dominated by two German Powers, and that they would be able to make sure of this by their well-practiced skill in playing Vienna and Berlin off against each other. Czechs, Slovenes, Croats and to a somewhat lesser extent Romanians, Slovaks, and Poles became more and more convinced that Austria-Hungary had become an instrument of Pangermanism, and that they could be saved only by the breakup of the monarchy, to be achieved with the help of other powers, especially Russia or France.

Though this discussion concerns the Danubian lands only, it may be worth noting that rather similar processes were taking place during these decades in the Russian Empire. There also, in the greater part of the nineteenth century, loyalty to the Emperor was all that was required of the subject. Tsar Nicholas I refused to permit pressure to be placed on loyal Baltic Germans, Finns, or Armenians to turn them into Russians; and consented to the persecution of Poles not because they were Poles instead of Russians, but because they were seditious subjects who had rebelled against their Tsar. This changed toward the end of the century as a result of forces not unlike those operating in Austria-Hungary. The soldiers were worried about the security of frontiers inhabited by non-Russians. The Orthodox Church was eager to convert Protestants, Catholics, and Moslems to the true faith. The numbers of bureaucrats were growing as estates diminished in size and it became difficult to find properties for noblemens' children. Bureaucrats believed in the virtues of uniformity and disliked diversity. Those who had liberal inclinations (and this was by no means unknown) favored centralization and opposed regional autonomies. In all these matters Russian development resembled Hungarian rather than Austrian. The result—the policy of Russification adopted under Alexander III and Nicholas II—was strikingly similar to Magyarization and was counterproductive in exactly the same way. Polish, Ukrainian, Tatar, Baltic, and other nationalisms flourished as a result of Russification, in just the same way as Slovak, Romanian, and Serbian nationalisms flourished in Hungary.

The immediate cause of the First World War was the murder by a Bosnian Serbian student of the heir to the

Habsburg throne, Archduke Franz Ferdinand. The conventional wisdom, firmly embedded in the school history books, is that the assassination was "just the occasion" for the outbreak of the war, which had been truly caused by "deeper conflicts."

But was not the clash between conflicting nationalisms in Central Europe a "deep conflict?" The South Slav problem, which produced Gavrilo Prinsip, was only one of them. I have spoken at some length of the German-Czech conflict. There was also a Polish problem involving the relations between the German, Austrian, and Russian empires; a Romanian problem involving Austria and Russia; a problem of Greater Greece involving not only Greece and Turkey but also Italy, Russia, France, and Britain. For the aspirant nations, these conflicts between nationalisms subsumed all the issues familiar in European history since the eighteenth century—constitutional, social, and ideological. The Bosnian Serbs may appear to the Olympian gaze of a modern liberal historian as a tawdry lot of petty bandits defying a great civilized empire; they were no more and no less tawdry and petty than the piratical English sailors who defied glorious civilized Spain, or the country bumpkins of Concord, Massachusetts, who defied King George III. Conflicts between Danubian nations, affecting some two hundred million people, were no more superficial than the conflicts which convulsed Western Europe from 1789 onward. They resulted from the extension eastward of the problems brought about by the Enlightenment, the rise of industrial capitalism, the class struggle, and the urban mass society. They really cannot be disposed of by the fav-

23

orite scapegoats of present-day journalists or historians. They were not conjured up by the fanatic Prinsip, or the Machiavellian Poincaré and Izvolsky, or the militarist Ludendorff, or poor senile Franz Josef. They were an exhalation from the lives of millions of half-peaceful, half-frustrated citizens. The small men and women were no more guiltless lambs than the statesmen were ravening wolves. All these things entered into the complex of conflicts which we call the nationalisms of Central Europe. These, far more than Anglo-German naval or commercial rivalry, or bitterness about Alsace-Lorraine, are the origins of the "heart sickness" from which Europe still suffers. Nineteen fourteen marked the first time that the conflicts of the Danube lands plunged half the human race into catastrophe.

The catastrophe began with war, but war did not end it, as we shall see later. In the war the two German powers, as their leaders now clearly regarded themselves, went from strength to strength. Militant Germanity seemed invincible. Austrian and Prussian soldiers marched "shoulder to shoulder," to quote the official public relations phrase mercilessly repeated in later years of disillusion by the great Austrian satirist Karl Kraus in his bizarre drama *The Last Days of Humanity*. Marching shoulder to shoulder, Austrian and Prussian soldiers brought the great Russian Empire to its knees, and then they fell on their own knees. Millions lost their lives, their homes or their countries. Princes and statesmen bemoaned the fate which had overtaken them and plaintively proclaimed their innocence. Small men, faceless members of the crowd in great cities on ethnic borderlands, also worried about these things. One was a Bohemian corporal who had served bravely not in his own but in the Reich's army. He had been an unsuccessful student of painting in Vienna, and had never had any fixed profession or training. He had grown up in the frenzy of race hatred that was one essential feature of the culture of the capital of the Habsburg Monarchy, the great and beautiful city of Vienna. The race hatred was the obverse of the medal whose other side proudly bore the features of Freud and Hofmannsthal and Wittgenstein and many other famous faces. The name of this frustrated artist and patriot was Adolf Hitler.

The Interlude
of Small States

The view that the collapse of the Habsburg Monarchy was followed by an age of barbarism, punctuated by varying periods of civilized life in some regions, as well as the fact that there was another side to this matter has already been mentioned. The other side is of course that the breakup of the three empires, and the emergence of new or enlarged, but comparatively small, national states was felt by millions to be a marvelous liberation, and that the new period in the Danubian lands was greeted with tremendous optimism, by most of the nations concerned and by their foreign well-wishers. This was the time when the Wilsonian message of self-determination was hailed as a secular gospel. (I do not know who first coined the phrase, Lenin certainly used it well before 1918, but it was without doubt Wilson who popularized it throughout the world.) This was also a time for enthusiastic constitution-making, France being the principal model, a time when men were convinced that if you had the right constitution down on paper, liberty and progress were yours. It is easy for us now to condemn those men and women as naïve, but the historian, whose job is to understand and record moods as well as events, states of mind as well as statistics, cannot—or at least should not—afford himself the luxury of sarcastic hindsight. Besides, how much hindsight does our generation possess? Some forms of naïveté die hard. It was not only in the age of Wilson that special virtues were ascribed to new states and small nations, or that power politics, balances of power, and secret negotiations were proclaimed as bad practices of the past, now abandoned for ever. I can think of an eminent politician or two in my own country who to this very day cherishes—or at least loudly asserts that he cherishes—these illusions, and it is not hard to think of one or two from other countries.

The new governments in the new states, or at least in several of them, quickly set about doing some admirable things. Political parties and political newspapers proliferated. Land reforms were enacted; great lands belonging to rich—and not only rich—noblemen were divided among the peasants. Efforts were made to start new industries, and to improve those which already existed; various forms of encouragement were devised both for indigenous business talent and for foreign capitalists. Particular attention was given to education. Already before 1918 the small Balkan states —Serbia, Bulgaria, and Greece—had a rather good record in building schools, though perhaps they were more concerned with quantity than with quality. Austria, Bohemia, Moravia, and the city of Budapest already had school systems equal to the best European standards. In rural Hungary, Romania, and most of

27

Poland this was not the case; after 1918, however, great efforts were made in all these lands to get the people to school.

Nevertheless, looking back at the period as a whole, and considering how it began and how it ended, the picture remains more somber than bright; and though we must never forget the achievements, my emphasis will, I fear, be on the darker side.

In the first place, the bitterness of the defeated must be mentioned. First come the Germans, including those in the Reich, whose boundaries had been drastically reduced, and outside it, in Austria, where a majority now desired union with Germany. (This statement should be modified only by the fact that the public eagerness of the main political parties in Austria for union, or *Anschluss,* varied according to whether the corresponding party was in or out of power in the Weimar Republic at the time.) And most of all, there were those large German communities which were placed under the rule of Czechs or Poles or Romanians or Serbs. Then there was the bitterness of Italy, whose nationalists felt that, though Italy had gained territory, she had not got enough. The bitterness of these nationalists, the indecision of Catholic democrats and socialists on this issue, and the rise of bands of Italian nationalist irregular troops on the frontier between Italy and Yugoslavia had a lot to do with Mussolini's rise to power, and from the first, Mussolini was resolved to magnify tension in the Danube lands and profit from it. Thirdly, there was the bitterness of Hungarians, of whom about one third now lived under foreign rule, in Slovakia, in northeastern Yugoslavia (or Vojvodina) and above all in Transylvania, where more than a million and a half Magyars came under the rule of some three million Romanians. Fourthly, most of the Bulgarian people believed strongly that the people of Macedonia, which had been kept together with Serbia and incorporated in the new state of Yugoslavia, were and wished to remain Bulgarians. Finally, there was the unknown factor of Soviet Russia, distant and veiled in obscurity, partly of its own making and partly the result of boycott by the capitalist world, yet still to be reckoned with in some sense as the heir to the empire of the tsars. All these embittered and defeated nations contained strong movements determined to "redeem" the lost lands (irredentists) or to revise the peace treaties (revisionists). To sum up, though the new frontiers did very largely conform to Wilson's self-determination principle, though they corresponded much more closely to the boundaries which separated nations from each other than had the frontiers of the old empires, it is probably true to say nevertheless that after 1919 a greater volume of effective nationalist discontent existed in the Danube lands than before.

In addition to the bitterness of the defeated nations, the great social and economic problems, which had formed the foundation of the discontents of the pre–1914 era, were little, if at all, nearer to solution.

Land reform was altogether refused in Hungary. The revolution of 1918 against the old regime had been followed by a period of rule by communists, and this had been overthrown by foreign military intervention (mainly the Romanian army) and had led to an attempt to restore the old regime. The triumphant Hungarian landowners and bureaucrats were resolved to keep the land out of peasant hands, and to keep the peasants out of politics. Something like universal suffrage was enacted, but in rural constituencies the ballot was open —which meant that a peasant who voted against the nominee of the local landowners and officials did so at his own peril. In Poland there was not much land reform, chiefly because the political parties were too busy quarreling with each other to make up their minds on any important issue, until May 1926, when Marshal Joseph Pilsudski seized power. He was too concerned, however, at that stage of his long life, with national and military glory to bother himself with such trivialities.

In the other countries there were land reforms, but even these were less good than appeared on the surface. In the new lands which went to Czechoslovakia, Yugoslavia, and Romania, the great landowners were mostly foreigners, so nationalist as well as social motives favored the seizure of their estates. But the land went mostly only to those local peasants who belonged to the victorious nation. Thus, for example, in Slovakia not many of the poor Hungarian peasants and landworkers who lived on a Hungarian estate received any land; that went almost entirely to Slovak peasants. The honorable exception was Romania. Here not only Hungarian and Russian landowners in the new lands, but also Romanian landowners in the Old Kingdom lost a great deal of land. Even so, the number of Magyar peasants in Transylvania or of Ukrainian peasants in Bessarabia or Bukovina who received land was rather small.

More important in the longer term was that far too little was done to help the new peasant landowners to become efficient farmers. The governments did not of course have very large revenues, but too little of what they did have went into improving agriculture. They were understandably concerned with industry, but the effective industrial programs left much to be desired. A good deal of the available resources went either to corruption or to unproductive administrative controls. Industrial progress suffered from the tension between the ruling political parties, those national or religious minorities who were disproportionately successful in business (above all Jews and Germans), and the foreign capitalists whom the governments simultaneously sought to attract and resented. Another difficulty was the constant use by politicians of new business enterprises as places to fill with jobs for the boys.

Finally, the educational system was poisoned by nationalist demagogy. In the schools history consisted to a large extent of nationalist mythology, each nation was taught that it embodied the virtues of western (chiefly French, and to some extent, German or Italian or English) culture, and that all its neighbors were barbarians, to be treated with contempt or at best with indifference. At the university level, of course, a great deal of splendid work was achieved, and there were many great scholars and brilliant students; yet the prevalent impression was one of nationalist frenzy and hatred. At the worst, university students became recruits to the strong-arm squads which went around smashing Jewish shops, or fighting each other in the streets. Some proved their patriotic virtues by assassinating unpopular politicans; and the judges and juries were often so infected with the current frenzy, or so afflicted with guilt complexes toward these noble young people for whom their generation had failed to provide a country worthy for heroes to live in, or simply so afraid of other assassins' bullets, that they let them off with nominal penalties.

I earlier, tried to show that in Austria the basis of the legitimacy of government was loyalty to the dynasty, and in Hungary to the Magyar nation, and that both forms of legitimacy had failed in the end to satisfy their subjects. In the Danube lands between the wars, the old Hungarian form of legitimacy essentially became universal. All were regarded as national states, with one official nation (in German, *Staatsvolk*). Minority treaties, registered with the League of Nations, protected the rights of communities of different language or religion to maintain schools and churches of their own and to promote the general development of their own culture. However, the governments and party leaders were most unwilling to admit that their subjects of different speech or faith belonged to another nation, and that the majority of that nation lived in a neighboring state. Thus, Romanian politicans had no objection to Transylvanian Magyars speaking Magyar and being educated in school in the Magyar language, but they did object to their considering themselves as members of the Magyar nation, the majority of which lived in the neighboring state of Hungary rather than as Romanians of Magyar speech. The Romanian politicians suspected them of loyalty to another, and hostile, state; and in this they were often quite right, just as in prewar Hungary, the Magyar politicians' fear that their Slovak subjects had Panslav, or their Romanian subjects had Daco-Romanian sympathies came to be justified. In two countries only, after 1918, did the problem of national minorities and of official nationalism not cause serious trouble: in Hungary and Bulgaria. The reason was of course that both these countries had been reduced to such small dimensions that their populations were almost nationally homogeneous; there was a German minority in Hungary and a Turkish minority in Bulgaria, but they were rather small. However, in the other countries this was far from the case. The *Staatsvolk* in Romania amounted at most to 70 percent of the population, and perhaps to not much more than 60 percent. In Poland the proportion was a little lower. Both these were of course majorities, as compared with the actual minority position of the Magyars in pre–1918 Hungary and Croatia, but to have a third of the population alienated from the states was still a dangerous condition.

In two countries, Czechoslovakia and Yugoslavia, there was a special situation. Here it was claimed that there was one *Staatsvolk*, but this was a mere fiction.

The Czechoslovak nation existed only in the imagination of a fairly large number of Czech and of a few Slovak politicians. There was a Czechoslovak state, and this had come into being because almost all Czechs and Slovaks wanted it. But the Slovaks were a separate nation, and considered the Czechs a brother nation but not the same as themselves. The well-meant efforts of Czech officials and intellectuals to raise the Slovaks from their admittedly backward level up to the level of the Czech nation often produced more hard feelings than gratitude, and when the would-be benefactors made it clear that in their view the new Czechoslovak nation consisted simply of the Czech nation, and that the aim was to turn Slovaks into Czechs, the Slovak reaction grew more and more bitter, until a large part of the Slovak nation supported a nationalist movement which regarded the Czechs as the national enemy, in the same sense in which before 1918 they had regarded the Magyars as the national enemy.

In Yugoslavia things were much worse. A strong movement had existed before 1914 which was aimed at the union of all Serbs, Croats, and Slovenes in a single state. A slogan used by many of its leaders was that they were one nation of three names (*jedan troimeni narod*). The story of the relationship of this movement to the Habsburg Monarchy and to the kingdom of Serbia, and of its activities both at home and in exile during the First World War are far too complex to discuss here; it must suffice to say that the common state was set up in 1918, and that there were from the first very deep disagreements as to whether it should be federal or unitary, and what should be the relationship between Serbs and Croats (not to mention Slovenes, Macedonians, and Moslems of Serbo-Croatian speech). Bitter disputes raged in the new parliament, and in June 1928 the Croatian leader Stepan Radić was shot on the floor of the House by another member. At this point cooperation between Serbs and Croats broke down completely, and King Alexander proclaimed a dictator-ship. His idea was to use the army to force everyone to regard himself not as a Serb or Croat or Slovene or Macedonian, but as a Yugoslav. There was to be just one Yugoslav nation, comprising about 85 percent of the population of the state. But the truth was that the dictatorship was run by Serbian gendarmes and army officers, and that the Yugoslav nation was simply the Serbian nation writ large. This meant that the legiti-macy of government was based on about 40 percent of the population—a still lower proportion than that of old Hungary. In reality, even the 40 percent was exag-gerated, because a large part of the Serbian nation, especially of its educated class, detested and rejected the regime.

One more point about the political structure de-serves a few words. Four of these states—Poland, Czechoslovakia, Romania, and Yugoslavia—were formed by putting together territories which had for centuries enjoyed quite different forms of government. I am thinking not so much of political doctrines as of administrative practice—how government impinged on the lives of individual townsmen and farmers. Broadly speaking there had been four types of government: Austrian, Hungarian, Russian, and Turkish. The Austrian may be said to have been incorrupt, based on respect for the law and a humane attitude toward the individ-ual (even though many Austrian bureaucrats were cold fish, dry as dust and awkward to deal with, as many English bureaucrats are today—and perhaps this is not unknown farther west still). Of the Hungarian type one may perhaps say that it was fairly incorrupt, was based on the manipulation and distortion of the law, and showed scant regard for the humanity of its subjects unless they were socially well connected. It bore some relationship to the Austrian prototype, but we may perhaps say that it was rather a pale copy, or that it paid to the Austrian type the tribute of vice to virtue. Russian administration, at least in the borderlands with which we are concerned (eastern Poland and Bessarabia), was incompetent, corrupt, and brutal. Ottoman administration, in the last decades of the empire, was probably even worse. All the same, it is only fair to the Turks to note that in Macedonia, with warring bands of irregular fighters, subsidized from neighboring states and shooting both at the Turks and at each other, it would have been hard even for a team of angels to run a good administration.

Now, in the successor states the distribution of power between the more advanced and more backward regions varied according to three patterns. The first was that the people of the more advanced region held power over the more backward. This was the case in Czechoslovakia, where the "Austrian-trained" Czechs ruled over the "Magyar-trained" Slovaks. This largely accounts for the fact that, with all its faults, Czechoslovakia remained for its twenty years existence a civilized, free, and democratic state. This was not true in Poland, where the people of the most advanced region (that which had been under Prussian rule, which by my criteria was better still than Austrian), and the "Austrian-trained" Galicia were before long subjected to rule by their "Russian-trained" compatriots. In Romania and Yugoslavia the more backward regions, with an Ottoman tradition modified by fifty years or so of Europeanization, dominated those which had an "Austrian" or "Magyar" background. The third and worst type of situation was in two provinces where officials of this latter type (shall we call them "Balkan-trained"?) ruled over people who had just escaped from Russian or Ottoman rule, that is, in Bessarabia under Romania, and in Macedonia under Yugoslavia.

All these troubles and defects which I have listed were immensely intensified in the 1930s with the onset of the world economic depression. The bottom fell out of the agricultural market. Peasants were crushed by debt. The growing pressure of population on resources, which had been felt more and more in every past year, added progressively to the misery. The disproportion between the prices of farm goods and those townmade goods which were necessities for the peasants (the so-called "price scissors") widened sensationally. The result was massive unemployment and poverty.

In industry things were hardly better. Unemployment was more visible, and so aroused more public polemics. It was most striking in the longest developed industrial region of the Danube Basin—the Bohemian borderlands. Here the workers were German and the government Czech. It is not surprising that Germans felt that the government in Prague was neglecting them because they were Germans. It was of no use to point out that some of the troubles of German Bohemian industry were due to obsolescent methods (as was, for example, the case in many of the staple industries in Britain in these years), and that the relatively better condition of some Czech-owned industries in the interior of Bohemia was due to more up-to-date business methods. The German workers were convinced of national discrimination, and deserted in flocks the ranks of the socialist and communist parties to join the *Sudetendeutsche Partei* of Konrad Henlein, modeled on Hitler's National Socialist Party and subsidized by him.

The slump also bitterly affected the professional classes. Danubian universities had long suffered from overproduction of lawyers. There were few jobs left for the new graduates. This problem was particularly bad in Hungary, because there were thousands of Magyars who had been bureaucrats in territories which had passed to neighboring countries. Not only did these people have to be looked after, but by the 1930s their children had grown up and were looking for jobs too. In the successor states larger numbers, if they belonged to the *Staatsvolk*, were absorbed into the expanding bureaucracy, which somehow had to be paid from dwindling government resources. Others tried to go into business. Children of gentry families abandoned the old prejudice that money-grubbing was something with which a gentleman could not soil his hands. But the trouble was that the jobs were not there. In a large part of the region, the jobs were in the hands of Jews. The same was true of the free professions, especially of medicine, the law, and the press. In these professions Jews had made good careers at a time when the children of the majority nations had been indifferent to them (if they came from the higher classes) or unable through lack of education to rise into them (if they had been peasants). But now it was widely believed that

Jewish predominance in commercial and cultural activities was due to a sinister Jewish conspiracy to undermine the nation and enslave it to sinister international forces. Anti-Semitic orators won mass audiences. At the same time governments struggled to create new industries, manned essentially by bureaucrats and with a labor force recruited from peasant ranks, supported by government subsidies. The new bureaucratic business class, together with the old bureaucracy, began to press for discriminatory laws against Jews.

All these disastrous trends contributed to the growth of Fascism—of the indigenous movements which can be so described and of the influence of the Italian and German regimes.

The word Fascism was adopted for his party by Benito Mussolini (though the word *fascio,* from which it is derived, had been used by agrarian socialists in Italy at the beginning of the century). Mussolini, who started his political life as a left-wing socialist, was essentially an old-style dictator, who cultivated the style of a Renaissance *condottiere* but made good use of the most modern techniques of propaganda and repression. He was good at rhetoric, and invented some fine, resonant words, like *totalitario,* but only partly put them into practice. His chief function in Danubian history, the main result of his intrigues with Hungary and Bulgaria against Yugoslavia and France, was to keep the discontents and hatred alive, to keep the Danubian ovens at a good temperature until the master chef arrived, who knew what dishes he was going to cook. This was of course Adolf Hitler.

Hitler was the heir to the anti-Semitic Greater German imperialism of the ethnic borderlands of Austria, which I have already discussed. His aim was a vast Great German Third Reich, that was to achieve all the aims that had been entertained by the most imaginative expansionists of both Austria and Prussia. He looked still farther. He proposed to annex vast tracts of European Russia, to colonize Germans and partly destroy and partly enslave the people who already lived there. He proceeded by stages. He first played on the guilt complex of the British and French public about the injustice of the Versailles settlement, in order to introduce conscription and to send his troops over to the demilitarized left bank of the Rhine. Then he brought Austria, and then the Bohemian and Moravian borderlands "back into the Reich." Here too the Western guilt complex (which incidentally was also widely developed in America too, though the United States had no active part to play in these events) enabled him to work his will without opposition from any great power.

Meanwhile he was making friends and influencing people in the Danube lands. To the irredentists of Hungary and Bulgaria he promised a reordering of frontiers, from which they hoped to achieve their dreams. To the nationalist middle classes in countries with large Jewish populations he appealed as their liberator from Jewish corruption; as the man who would see to it that Hungarians and Romanians and Poles would get the jobs in business and in the professions that were held by Jews; as the champion of integral nationalism, the man who would help them to purify their nations from alien elements. Hitler's anti-Semitism was something which turned people against him in France, England, and America—even those persons who from guilt complex or other motives were well disposed to the German nationalist point of view. But in the Danube lands, anti-Semitism was something which won Hitler friends, which brought him mass support, in the middle classes and to a lesser extent among peasants and workers, not in all the Danubian nations and not in quite the same social groups in each nation, but to some extent, in most of the region. He also won friends by his economic policies. The German market was opened to the farm goods and raw materials of the Danube lands whose producers had been so cruelly hit by the depression. The Germans did well out of this revived trade, but so also did the Danubians, including peasants and workers no less than merchants and industrialists.

Another important success of Hitler, and of the fascist movements which, with some support from Hitler, became strong in Hungary and Romania, and to a lesser extent in Slovakia and Croatia, was his appeal to youth. The National Socialists claimed to be the party of Youth. Handsome blond marching boys and girls—that was the new Germany. Hitler had abolished the System (one of his favorite words). The old men, with their constitutions and their due process of law and their dreary papers and formalities and their mean cowardly preference for reason over glorious exalting Action, were out; German Youth would think with its blood, and march forward with quiet firm step (*mit ruhig festem Schritt*). Some readers will remember those words from the Horst Wessel song; or Mussolini's party anthem: "*Giovinezza, giovinezza, primavera della*

41

bellezza" (Youth, youth, springtime of beauty). The great British journalist Eric Gedye described in March 1938 the scenes in Vienna at the *Anschluss.* Crowds lined the streets welcoming the Fuhrer. On the same streets handsome youths in newly acquired Nazi uniforms made elderly Jews scrub the sidewalks and kicked them as they stooped down to do it. A few years later these and other youths began to march with quiet firm step, first west then east. Their graves stretch all the way back from Stalingrad to Berlin.

Militant fascist movements arose in two Danubian states, Romania and Hungary. These regarded themselves as revolutionary movements; they wanted to overthrow the whole existing regime, destroy the power not only of the Jews but also of the indigenous capitalists and landowners, and bind their countries to Hitler's Third Reich. Because these militant fascists were so hostile to the existing regimes, the existing regimes persecuted them, in Romania very brutally, in Hungary rather mildly. They never obtained power by their own efforts. The Romanian fascists, the so-called Iron Guard, were brought into the government in September 1940 as a direct result of the partition of Transylvania, by Germany and Italy, between Romania and Hungary. This was in turn a direct result of the German victory over France in 1940. The Iron Guard had to share power with a conservative Romanian general, Ion Antonescu. The partners soon quarreled, and Hitler had to choose between them. It was more important for him to have the Romanian army for the war which he was planning in Russia than to see his ideological disciples in power. So he chose Antonescu, and Antonescu bloodily suppressed the Iron Guard, thereby incidentally saving hundreds of thousands of Romanian Jewish lives. In Hungary, the existing regime cooperated, a little reluctantly and very inefficiently, with Hitler in his Russian war. When Hitler lost his patience with the Hungarian rulers, who were secretly negotiating with his British and American enemies to get out of the war, he took the country over with his armed forces, but still he did not put the Hungarian fascists in power. Instead, he made use of the most extreme pro–German wing of the old regime. It was only when Head of State Admiral Horthy (an admiral without a navy in a kingdom without a king) made another attempt to get out of the war, that Hitler brought the Hungarian fascists in, in October 1944. But then the war was already lost. It was too late to do anything except to make all Hungary a battlefield and Budapest a heap of ruins.

So the really strong fascist movements inside the Danube states did not in fact play a very important part. Instead, from the mid–1930s, the Danubian governments began to ape Hitler's and Mussolini's rhetoric, and began to try to maneuver between France, Britain, Germany, and Italy.

The exception was Czechoslovakia. Its leader, President Beneš, hardly had a choice. His only hope was alliance with France and Russia, the combination which had brought the Czechs their independence in 1918. In 1938 this alliance broke down, because the French were divided and war-weary; the British government thought the German claims on Czechoslovakia were justified, and pulled the French back; and Stalin was

43

busy exterminating half his officer corps in the Great Purge. So there was the surrender at Munich, and war was postponed for a year.

The Polish leaders, by contrast, were willing to go a long way with Hitler. Hitler, whose brand of German imperialism was of the Austrian, rather than the Prussian kind, did not originally hate the Poles. Russia, not Poland, was his main enemy, and he even hoped to have the Poles as allies against Russia—as Napoleon had had, and Franz Josef as well in 1914. So Hitler made a treaty of nonaggression with Poland in 1934, and then in 1939 made the Poles what he thought was a very generous offer. They need only give him some small bits of territory, and then they could be his partners in conquering the Ukraine. But the Polish leaders, though willing enough to ape fascist rhetoric, absolutely refused to give up any territory, and they had no desire at all to go to war in the Ukraine. So they rejected his offer, and he destroyed them, having first made a robber's bargain with Stalin at their expense. This started off the Second World War.

Now the invasion of Poland, many may think, was only the occasion, and not the cause of the Second World War. My answer to that is the same as to the similar belief about the Sarajevo assassination and the First World War. If Poland had not been the immediate cause, then Romania or Hungary or Yugoslavia or Greece would have been. All these lands were objects of Hitler's ambitions, and all were torn by national and social conflicts. Hitler's determination to seize the Danube lands, and ultimately to proceed to invade Russia from this territorial base, was as much the cause of the Second World War as the national conflicts in the Danube lands had been the cause of the First World War. Of course it is true that after 1941, with the invasion of Russia and the Japanese attack on Pearl Harbor, the war became truly world-wide, but that is another story. My point is that the national and social conflicts—inextricably mixed with each other—in the Danube lands were the major causes of the war which began in 1939.

What actually happened in the Danube lands is well known but needs to be summarized. Hitler got Austria, then German Bohemia, and then all the Czech lands without firing a shot. He then quickly conquered Poland, dividing it up with his ally Soviet Russia. In the summer of 1940 he made Romania and Hungary his allies, and shortly afterwards, Bulgaria. In March 1941 he got the Yugoslav government to sign an alliance with him, but a few days later a few Serbian air force officers overthrew this government. Hitler then attacked and quickly conquered Yugoslavia, and carved it up into nine different chunks. Meanwhile Mussolini had attacked, and then been beaten by, the Greeks, and so Hitler's army had to conquer Greece too. By the summer of 1941 all the Danube lands, and the lands to the north and south of them, were in Hitler's hands, and he was ready for his Russian campaign.

It is a sad story, and the record of the various Danubian governments is not very inspiring. However, I think that if we expend our indignation on blaming them for not resisting Hitler more efficiently, or for not realizing what a monster he was (with the exception of the Czechoslovak government, which was simply betrayed by its ally and its ally's ally), we are wasting our time. They did their best, by the diplomatic standards of the time, with the defense forces available to them, and their best was not good enough. As to the failure to recognize Hitler as a monster, they shared this failure with almost all the leading statesmen of the West, on both sides of the Atlantic.

As for Hitler's monster quality, this too needs a few words here. Poles were deported like cattle, terrorized, deprived of their educated class and their school system, and at times slaughtered. Appalling massacres were committed in Yugoslavia both by Germans and by Yugoslav fascists. Russian prisoners of war were allowed to die of starvation by the hundreds of thousands.

The most terrible of all Hitler's crimes was of course his "final solution" for the Jews, who had played so great a part in the economy and culture of the Danube lands, especially in the two great cities of Vienna and Budapest. About six million perished in the extermination centers in Poland. Some perhaps think that that bare statistic is enough, but I think it would not be amiss to bring the statistic alive by referring to a scene from real life. It comes from the report of the anti-Nazi German mining engineer Kurt Gerstein, who got a job in the SS in a camp to see for himself what was happening, then tried to get the facts known in the outer world, without success, and ended his days in imprisonment in France as a war criminal. The full report is published in the first number of the Munich historical periodical *Vierteljahreshefte für Zeitgeschichte.* Gerstein described how batches of 750 men, women, and children were packed naked into chambers of forty-five cubic meters, how they were kept waiting in this state for two hours and forty-nine minutes until the gas could be turned on; and how thirty-two minutes later the last victim was dead. Nowadays demagogues in the United Nations and in the streets of Western cities love to throw at each other the word "genocide" as a form of vulgar abuse. Let us remember what genocide was.

A special word perhaps for the Jews of Hungary. They had been so well treated under the old regime before 1918 (for its own reasons) that most of those who in 1918 became citizens of Romania, Czechoslovakia, or Yugoslavia continued to regard themselves as Magyars, thereby bringing on themselves the understandable dislike of the newly dominant nations and the new governments. Between 1939 and 1941, when Hungary recovered a large part of these territories, the Jews who lived in them were glad to become Magyar citizens again. When Hungary had a new census in 1941, these Jews gladly registered as Magyars, thereby swelling the statistics of the Hungarian nation as desired by the rulers. Less than three years later these Jews were deported in train after train to the extermination camps in Poland. And the orders were given, not by fascist fanatics but by a government whose strongest personality was the highly respectable banker Bela Imredy, who had many good friends in London and New York. It is true that the Jews of Budapest itself escaped this fate, and merit should here be given to Admiral Horthy, the head of state.

It is a terrible irony that the Hungarian Jews, with a secure and honored place under the Hungarian old regime, before 1914 and again under Count Stephen Bethlen in the 1920s, should have been unimpressed by the efforts of other Jews to turn bits of Turkish swamp or desert into a new homeland. They belonged to Hungarian culture, indeed they largely created it. The great sociologist Oszkár Jászi, writing in 1917, was convinced that when the gross social inequalities were removed, and Hungary became a democratic state, the "Jewish question" would disappear. He could see no sense in Zionism. It is true that Hungary did not become a democratic state between the world wars, yet the government of 1944 was certainly much more democratic than the prewar governments, or Bethlen's government; it introduced the secret ballot in the villages, and the landowners lost most of their power. Yet the government to which Imredy belonged sent the trains off to the extermination centers, and the Jews who cultivated Turkish swamps not only survived but flourished exceedingly.

Today the city of Vienna is prosperous and as beautiful as ever. Its three hundred thousand Jews and their descendants are not there. I love to go there, as I used to love going there in the 1930s, and I have friends there. But I cannot quite forget the scene described by my friend Eric Gedye—the handsome young Austrian Nazis kicking elderly Jews in the Kärntnerstrasse, within sight of St. Stephen's spire.

Not everything was dark in the Danube lands in the 1930s. I remember Romanian friends in Transylvania who believed that their land, a land of ancient Romanian culture and ancient Magyar culture, could be a bridge between the two nations. I remember Croats and Serbs who believed that a Yugoslavia of brother nations could be a reality, and fought for it in four years of resistance against its conquerors. I remember the German Social Democrats from western Bohemia, enemies of Henlein's Bohemian Nazis and daily threatened by them, with whom as a guest (I had just graduated from Oxford). I marched through the streets of Pilsen in July 1938 to a meeting with Czech Social Democrats to pledge their loyalty to the Czechoslovak republic. Crowds of Czechs lined the streets, many ranks deep, calling out, "Long live our German friends." These people did not control policy, but they too have their place in history.

Hitler's thousand-year Reich collapsed, leaving Poland and Hungary, Bosnia, and Slovakia in ruins. Often in history there appear, in the abomination of desolation, not only despair but also soaring hopes and utopian longings. In 1945 the old order was destroyed and discredited. Surely there could be no return to the past, many people reasoned. Now at last must come a new deal, an end to national hatreds, brutal abuse of power, and abject poverty. To many thinking people who had no systematic knowledge of political or economic theory, the word "socialism" symbolized the belief and desire that the sacrifices should not have been vain. Even after they had seen Russian soldiers wreak their vengeance on Danubian cities, many of these people still put their faith in the leaders of the first socialist republic in the world.

It remains to be seen what has become of their hopes.

The New Empire

At the end of the Second World War all the Danubian lands except Bavaria and western Austria were controlled by a single great power whose center of gravity lay outside the Danube valley. One power held Europe from the east up to the Elbe and the Alps, thus overshadowing all forces based within Europe. Thus, the danger which all the great wars since the sixteenth century had been fought to prevent had come to pass. This preeminent power was known as the Union of Soviet Socialist Republics, and was the heir to the old Russian Empire.

This Russian dominance had in general terms been expected and accepted by the Western great powers. It is not my purpose now to enter into the ramifications of Allied diplomacy; the continuing study of that subject leads to repeated revision of important details, yet leaves the overall pattern little changed. Essentially, the Western leaders expected that victorious Soviet Russia would have a dominant influence on the foreign policy of all the governments that would emerge in the Danubian lands. The phrase "regimes friendly

51

to the Soviet Union" was widely used and widely approved as the aim of all the Allies. But this was all that was expected. It was believed that the restored states of this region would be sovereign over their own affairs, and that the will of the peoples would be ascertained and expressed by democratic processes. It may be that Western statesmen were foolish to expect this, but it remains true that most of them did, and that this was still more true of wider sections of public opinion. When the Soviet government behaved in a quite different manner, therefore, there was widespread alarm. This alarm, and the public indignation and official protests which resulted from it, did not, as some have since argued, constitute a betrayal by Western statemen of the bargain which they had made —leaving Greece to the British and the rest to the Russians. The nature of the earlier bargains is a matter of extreme complexity, and a subject of unsettled controversy, but in any case the bargains were not known to the thousands of European and American citizens who objected to Soviet behavior, and put pressure on the British and American governments, who could not have ignored it even had they wished.

What is beyond dispute is that for the Soviet rulers domination of foreign policy together with acceptance of real internal sovereignty was a policy acceptable in only one country—Finland. Elsewhere much more was demanded, and it can be briefly summed up in five points.*

* Let it be clear that these points are my summary in my own words, not a formal set of demands put forward from Moscow.

Firstly, all political parties that were not directly and fully controlled by a communist party must be suppressed. This meant that not only conservative but also radically leftist parties—in particular, the peasant parties and the social democrats—had to be suppressed. There was, in some cases, a transitional period during which the parties nominally still existed, but in fact their leaders were chosen and their organizations were managed, not by the membership of the parties but by the leaders of the communist party.

Secondly, friendship of an individual citizen with individual Americans, British, Frenchmen, or other West Europeans (other than persons approved by the communist parties of those countries), or still more the expression of any admiration for the policies of the two Western great powers (which were at that time still the fighting allies of the Soviet Union in the war), were to be treated as treasonable. Those guilty of such criminal attitudes were to be dismissed from their jobs, or imprisoned, or in some extreme cases killed, with or without trial. This was being put into effect in Romania, Bulgaria, and Poland in the winter of 1944-45, even while the war with Hitler was still going on.

Thirdly, the new governments were rapidly to re-mold their political institutions and administration so as to make them carbon copies of their Soviet equivalents. Among other things, that "peculiar institution" of the Soviet Union, the security police (Cheka, GPU, MVD, MGB, KGB, or whatever) was to be exactly copied, but was given a "native" name.

Fourthly, this process was to be carried out by persons chosen, trained, and controlled by Soviet officials. The leaders of the communist parties which now came to power in these countries either were themselves such persons or were obliged to act according to the orders of "advisers" assigned to them. There was one big exception, of which more later.

Fifthly, once the Soviet-type political order had been firmly established, then the economic and social policies and institutions of the Soviet Union were also to be introduced—collectivization, rapid industrialization, mobilization of labor—in the variations currently orthodox in Moscow.

The implementation of these five points put an end to the notion that a new deal for the Danubian peoples, a socialism to be designed by and for them, would take the place of the discredited old order. The old order was indeed gone, but in its place came an order designed by and for the new conquerors. Any heretical variations were ruthlessly punished. Only the new rulers knew what socialism was, and it was to be put into effect in their way. Only they knew what the words "regimes friendly to the Soviet Union" meant, and they were going to see to it that regimes of that kind were installed. Whether their motivation was their desire for security of Soviet territory, or an overweening conviction of their ideological correctitude, seems to me not only an unanswerable question, but a rather pointless one: in their minds the two sets of thinking were inextricably fused. Danubians holding socialist or revolutionary views who were not communists were given the opportunity to learn the new orthodoxies and practice the new obedience, and might hope thereby to be admitted in time into the new communist parties. If not, they could shut up; or they could go into exile (this option was open for the first year or two); or they could go to jail.

The pace of implementation of the new policies varied. It was rapid in Yugoslavia, Albania, and Bulgaria, a little slower in Poland and Romania, and took the longest to achieve in Hungary and Czechoslovakia.

However, already before this, in the early summer of 1948, a major crisis had occurred. It became plain that the existing leadership of the Yugoslav Communist Party was not acceptable to Stalin. Marshal Tito and his colleagues had fought their own war, and built their own state machine. Tito had ceased to be a minor Comintern official and had become a national leader. He felt loyalty to his people; and his people—and especially the communist officials among them—felt loyalty to him. Such a person could not, in the view of Joseph Stalin, be relied on, and such a system of power must be turned upside down. So the leaders of the Communist Information Bureau (Cominform) solemnly excommunicated Tito, and Stalin waited for the Yugoslav comrades to show their unbounded love of the Soviet Union, which they had endlessly proclaimed in the past, by getting rid of Tito and his clique. But nothing happened. The Yugoslav party remained loyal to its leader, and as for noncommunist Yugoslavs, they might not have liked Tito but they had no reason to exchange him for Stalin.

The failure to dislodge Tito was followed by Moscow-ordered purges of the other Danubian communist parties. Each party was given the task of "unmasking" some leaders guilty of "'nationalist deviationism." As in Moscow in the Great Purge of 1936-39, it was a matter of who got whom first. Victims were produced, and Moscow-style methods of interrogation, torture, and show trial were used. In 1951 a further category of suspects was added—persons of Jewish origin, who as such were liable to have relatives or contacts abroad, and were especially liable to the infection of Zionism. There were of course not many Jews left. Those who were left were not, I think, persecuted because they were Jews but because they were people of potentially divided loyalty, having relatives in the United States or Israel or elsewhere. Stalin and his Danubian followers were not, strictly speaking, anti-Semites, but when considered from the receiving end of the treatment, this became a rather academic consideration. The impact of the purges varied widely; it was most severe in Czechoslovakia and Hungary, the two most industrially advanced countries with long established social democratic parties of the Austrian type. In Czechoslovakia and Hungary about half the membership of the Central Committees of the communist parties was removed. The purge was milder in Bulgaria and Romania, and mildest of all in Poland.

The years of the purge were also very unpleasant for people who were not members of the communist party. In these years, under the impact of the Korean war, tremendous efforts were made to step up production in industry in general, and in heavy industry in particular. This goal was realized by squeezing the peasants through taxation and extracting more labor from the workers for the same or for lower real wages.

The death of Stalin in March 1953 brought a relaxation. Pressure on peasants to join collective farms was reduced, and many collectives were dissolved. Many political prisoners were released. Production of consumer goods increased and more freedom of expression was allowed outside the strictly political sphere— in the natural sciences, in literature, and even in economics. The relaxation coincided with a workers' revolt in the Czech city of Pilsen, and more widespread revolts in East Berlin and other large cities of eastern Germany; whether these were a cause of the relaxation or a response to it, is not an easy question to answer. The twentieth congress of the Communist Party of the Soviet Union in February 1956, at which Khrushchev made his famous speech denouncing the crimes of Stalin, naturally caused excitement in Eastern Europe, beginning with a workers' rising in Poznan in Western Poland in June, continuing with the crisis between Poland and the Soviet Union in October 1956, and culminating in the revolution in Hungary at the end of the same month.

There followed some years of reassertion of Soviet supremacy in the whole region. In 1955 and 1956 Khrushchev had encouraged increased sovereignty for the governments of the communist states, partly, I myself am inclined to think, as a result of an element of genuine belief that, if communist power were exercised in a more humane manner, and if more regard were paid to national sensibilities, the peoples themselves would genuinely accept it. After the Hungarian Revolution this policy was partly reversed, and stronger

Soviet pressures were exerted on the Danubian Communist leaders. However, the situation changed again when the independent policies of China began to alarm the Soviet rulers, and it began to seem necessary to purchase East European support against China by further concessions to sovereignty. The government which made best use of this situation was the Romanian, from 1962 onward. The situation became less favorable to the East European governments when China was reduced to chaos by the "Cultural Revolution." This was the misfortune of the reforming communists in Czechoslovakia, whose efforts to give communism "a human face" in the summer of 1968 provoked Soviet armed intervention and the announcement of the Brezhnev Doctrine, which will be discussed later. The Czechoslovak affair was not the last disorder to date. At the beginning of 1971 there were large-scale riots of shipyard workers in Polish ports, which led to a change in the leadership of the communist party; this time however no Soviet troops were sent in.

So much for a brief summary of the historical process, which is for the most part, familiar to most readers. These larger questions that must now be considered are these: the achievements of the new regimes, how have they affected the national conflicts in the Danube lands, and what relationship exists between the Danubian nations and the Soviet empire of which they form part.

If we compare the general economic and cultural conditions of the Danubian nations today and in the 1930s, it would be not only ungenerous but also disingenuous to deny that a great deal has been done to meet the needs that were so pressing in the earlier period.

Great industries have been created, and they are directed not by a miscellaneous collection of local and foreign business men but by central planners thinking in terms of the whole economy. The success is real, though we should not forget first, that there would certainly also have been great progress if there had been a mixed economy, partly planned and partly private, and that the price of central planning has been the rise of massive new official hierarchies whose methods lack flexibility and who are suspicious of anything that is new. Still, on the whole, I believe that they have gained. The sight of the Greek economy, based on mass tourism and vulgarity and with shocking discrepancies between wealth and poverty, does not make me very confident that private enterprise and foreign aid would necessarily have made a very good job of the economies lying to the north.

Secondly, the vast rural surplus of population has been largely absorbed into other occupation, and agriculture has been reorganized. Here I must confess that I am less impressed. Output of agricultural goods per head of population has remained rather low, and the collectivized system clearly does not arouse peasant enthusiasm. One should however note firstly that Polish and Yugoslav agriculture are not collectivized, and secondly that collective farms are by no means the same thing in every country or in every region of a single country—some are notably more successful, with a notably happier membership, than others. As for the rural surplus, we should remember that a large part of it has gone into overmanned administrative structures or into inefficient factories, where several workers do a job which ought to be performed by one man. This "concealed unemployment" certainly costs the economies of a good deal. We should also remember the hundreds of thousands of Yugoslavs who obtain temporary employment in Germany or Switzerland. If they stayed at home, not only would the economy not benefit from their remittances (the money which today they send back to their dependents at home), but there would also be a large army of unemployed.

Thirdly, the new regimes have massively developed education. Access to universities and higher technical institutes is open to millions who could not have hoped for it in the old times. Of course, there have been lowered standards, the quality of education is not as good as its quantity (this was also the case before 1945), and schools are used as instruments of indoctrination. However, they have had one enormously important consequence. The whole population has been drawn into a single whole.

In the 1930s in most of these countries there were two nations: a Europeanized upper stratum of perhaps 10 to 30 percent of the population, who lived and thought more or less the same way as their social counterparts in Germany or France, and the rest, who lived in an almost medieval world, ranging if you like from the eighteenth century French peasant to the nineteenth century Russian *muzhik*. Today there is only one nation. (I am speaking of course of the principal nation in each state, rather than of the still surviving national minorities. Nor am I suggesting that they all have the same political beliefs.) Urban values predominate in the villages, brought in by electricity and radio and better roads, as well as by mass literacy. School children are subjected to a uniform official ethos, which is a sort of amalgam of residual Marxism-Leninism with a national mythology—a mixture, like all mythologies, of historical truth and fiction. Of the two main ingredients, it is the national mythology, rather than the Marxist-Leninist phrases, which makes its mark. At the same time, the official treatment of religion has had its effects. In some countries religion has in fact lost ground, as a result partly of processes of secularization familar in the West and partly as a result of official pressure. Here its place has been taken by an *ersatz* religion, a substitute, the new pseudo-socialist nationalism. In other countries pressures have only strengthened religion—especially in Poland, probably also in Romania—and here religion has fused with nationalism, each strengthening the other. Over the region as a whole, I should hazard the guess that national feeling is at least as strong as in the 1930s. In short, the completion of the process of drawing the mass of the population into the nation—of spreading national consciousness down to the grass roots—has been completed under communist party rule, and not so much expressed as camouflaged by Marxist-Leninist rhetoric and slogans. In fact the old slogan of Stalin's time has become the very opposite of reality: culture is not "national in form and socialist in content," but "socialist in form and nationalist in content."

How has this affected the old national conflicts? Under socialism, it had been hoped, national conflicts would be resolved and nationalism disappear. At first it looked as if these hopes might be fulfilled, at least in some regions. The policy of the Romanian communist leaders in 1945 was to seek friendship with the Hungarians of Transylvania. They were given their own university in Cluj (Kolozsvár) side by side with the Romanian university. In the region of largest compact Hungarian population, the Székély district in southeastern Transylvania, a special Autonomous Hungarian Region was set up. These liberties and equalities were of course granted only within the limits of the communist political dictatorship and economic policies; but at least there was genuine good will, a genuine determination not to punish Hungarians for any reason which would not equally cause Romanians to be punished. For this the Romanian communists deserve credit, as do some left-wing noncommunists like my friend Petru Groza, who to this day, I was glad to see, has a piece of the Danube embankment in Budapest named after him, the first Romanian, surely, to be so honored in Hungary! Unfortunately, the promise was not maintained. The upsurge of Romanian nationalism, which followed the estrangement between Romania and the Soviet Union in 1963, also led to anti-Hungarian policies. The Hungarian university and the Hungarian Autonomous Region were abolished. In the 1970s conditions somewhat improved, but latent hostility between Romanians and Hungarians in Transylvania, and between the Romanian and Hungarian governments, remained strong.

The situation in Yugoslavia also appeared promising. King Alexander's idea of a unitary Yugoslav nation was scrapped. Six republics were set up. The Croatian republic included all the main Croatian lands. The Macedonians also had a republic, and the doctrine was now officially adopted that they were neither southern Serbs nor western Bulgars, but a distinct nation. Great efforts were made to create a written Macedonian language, to publish both original and translated literature in it, and to develop a new Macedonian national consciousness. Unfortunately, the Yugoslav promise was also not fully upheld. In the late 1960s national antagonisms, especially between Serbs and Croats, welled up again, and cast dangerous shadows on the future of Yugoslavia. Even so, it remained true that there had been progress by comparison with conditions before 1941.

Elsewhere the outlook was not promising. The Soviet leaders behaved not like socialists seeking to cure the ills of nationalism, but like imperial rulers manipulating nationalist passions to further their imperial aims. They played off Slovaks against Hungarians, and Czechs against Slovaks. When they had quarrelled with Yugoslavia, they did their best to arouse Bulgarian irredentist claims on Macedonia. This game of playing Bulgaria against Yugoslavia has continued, with periods of excitement alternating with periods of calm, from 1948 up to the present day.

The most striking case of Soviet manipulation of national hatred was of course in the relations of Poles and Czechs with Germans. The Czechs were encouraged to expel the three and one half million Germans from Bohemia and Moravia. This was done not in the heat of war, but in cold blood after the fighting had stopped, and without doubt, several hundreds of thousands of Germans perished in the process, as a result of Czech brutality. The Czechs had good reason indeed to hate the Germans, but one cannot avoid the sad truth that by behaving in this way they lowered themselves to the moral level of Hitler's National Socialists. The Poles, who had suffered incomparably more, expelled, mostly while the war was still on, not only the Germans who had lived in the old Poland, but also many millions who had lived between the old Polish border and the rivers Oder and western Neisse, which formed Poland's new western frontier. These actions of course created hatred on the German side, and the Soviet leaders and their Polish and Czech servants did all they could to magnify and to perpetuate this. Their aim was to create an unbridgeable chasm to separate the Poles and Czechs from the Germans, and also from the three Western powers which inevitably became in varying degree the protectors of reconstructed Western Germany, so as to make them entirely dependent on Soviet protection. All evidence of the change of heart among the German people, especially among the young people born since 1945, was passed over in silence. Chancellor Adenauer and his successors, as well as the leaders of the United States and other Western nations linked in the Atlantic Alliance, were represented either as bloodthirsty neo-Nazis seeking revenge, or as patrons of such persons. In Poland this propaganda even increased in the 1960s in a desperate effort to create a scapegoat to divert Polish hatred from its natural object—Russia, and from their own governor, Władysław Gomułka. Gomulka in 1956 had appeared to be both a Polish patriot and a man concerned to give his people greater liberty, but he had soon proved to be hardly less servile toward his Russian masters, and hardly less intolerant of dissent, than his predecessors. Keeping the anti-German hatred campaign going was the only way to retard his loss of popularity. And then, all this suddenly ceased. Mr. Brezhnev suddenly decided that he needed better relations with West Germany, probably mainly for economic reasons, but there may have been other grounds as well, though love of Chancellor Brandt was probably not one of them. Orders were then given to the Poles to call off their campaign and follow the Soviet line. Poor Gomułka did as he was told; this was one of the last things he did before he was pushed out of power by his comrades after the Polish shipyard workers' rising.

I should like to make clear, as far as my own views are concerned, that I welcome this better relationship between the Germans and their eastern and south-eastern neighbors. Many may have doubts about the reasons which brought it about, and the limits within which it will be allowed to work, but in itself it is a good thing. It also corresponds to the wishes of the Danubian peoples. There was ample evidence in the 1960s that Gomułka's anti-German long-playing record was bringing diminishing returns, and that individual Poles sought contacts with individual West Germans, and enjoyed them when they had them. This was still more true, from an early period, of the Czechs. It is incidentally interesting to note how many of the

65

Czech intellectuals or professional people who left Czechoslovakia in 1968 have found new homes in Germany, Austria or German-speaking Switzerland, rather than in French- or English-speaking countries. Looking back farther into history, we must recognize that German language, German culture, and German people have been for centuries part of the Danubian world, and that relations between them and their neighbors have been peaceful and fruitful for much longer than they have been warlike and bitter. This is perhaps less true of the Prussians in the north, whose heir is of course not Chancellor Brandt but Mr. Honegger, the faithful heir to Walter Ulbricht. And those Poles who still feel bitter about Germans are most bitter of all about Germans who act as servants of Russia. Elsewhere, in the Danube lands proper, there are of course traditions of hostility to Germans, but they are rather recent, dating mostly since 1848, or at least since the French Revolution.

The Russians, by contrast, have never been intimately bound up with the Danubian peoples. The only nation of the region—in its widest sense—with whom they have had much contact are the Poles. Russians and Poles have known each other well, and hated each other well, for centuries, and with good reason, I am afraid, for most of the time. There have been Russians who have known well the orthodox Balkan peoples of Slav speech, the Serbs and Bulgarians, but not very many. As for the other peoples of the Danube lands, mutual ignorance has been the rule. My statement is not disproved by the fact that Panslavism, involving the belief that Russians are loving elder brothers, long flourished among Slovaks and Croats, and above all Czechs. This emotion was based not on knowledge but on hope and imagination. When the Czechs met the Russians in real life—not the odd traveling Russian intellectual like Professor Pogodin in the 1840s, but Russians in the mass—fraternal love was not conspicuous. It did not happen very often; the last time was in 1968.

This brings me to my third main problem, the relationship of the Danube peoples to the imperial power. Officially this is today based on the so-called Brezhnev Doctrine. If socialism is in danger in any of the socialist states of Eastern Europe, it is the right and the duty of the other socialist states to help the endangered state to restore socialism. This has to be done regardless of whether the socialist leaders—that is to say, the leaders in power in the communist party—ask for the help or not. Whether socialism is in danger, is decided by the other socialist states' rulers, under the leadership of the Central Committee of the Communist Party of the Soviet Union. How do we know that the CC of the CPSU knows what are the true interests of socialism?

The answer is simple. On 7 November 1917 the Bolshevik party in the city of Petrograd, which at that moment enjoyed the support of the majority of the industrial workers of that city, seized control of the government of Russia, and after some three years of civil war the leaders of the insurrection made themselves masters of the whole country. Since that time the members of the Central Committee of the ruling party have appointed their successors, from whom the supreme leaders have from time to time emerged. The events of 7 November 1917 were not a mere insurrection, but the Great October Socialist Revolution, led by the great genius Lenin, who later transmitted his power to Stalin, also a great genius, from whom it has passed to others. The Central Committee, presided over by these various men, is the repository of exclusive and scientific Marxist-Leninist knowledge. The Central Committee collectively embodies the immanent interests of the workers of the whole world and directs the progress of humanity along the foreordained road through socialism to full communism.

We have come full circle. This is a doctrine of apostolic succession, similar to that which was the foundation of the divine right of monarchs, according to which Habsburgs and Romanovs ruled.

However, this is not all. Not only must the ideological infallibility of the CPSU be recognized, but all aspects of Soviet reality must be represented, in all forms of public expression in the Danube lands, according to the detailed requirements of the current orthodoxy, and lavishly praised. National history must be rewritten wherever it touched on Russian history, not only in the Soviet period but in the distant past. Thus Empress Catherine's treatment of Poland must be interpreted according to the views of the Central Committee of the CPSU today.

It is only fair to admit that one attempt at rewriting history and remolding culture was abandoned. After 1945 Romanians were forced to sever cultural relations with France and Italy, to play down the role of France in the liberation of the Romanian nation and to show that throughtout their history, the Romanians' best friend had been the great Russian people (even though it could be admitted that one or two Tsars had perhaps not always behaved impeccably). Attempts were even made to transform the usage of the Romanian language, stressing the words of Slav origin and minimizing those of Latin origin, the ultimate aim no doubt being to show that the Romanians were not "Latins" but "Slavs." This was given up in the mid-1960s, when the insistence by the Romanian communist leaders on Romania's economic and cultural sovereignty was accepted.

Contrast this with Czechoslovakia. President Thomas Masaryk, the outstanding figure in twentieth-century Czech history, during a rather full life of eighty-seven years, spent a few months in Russia after the Bolshevik Revolution, during which he came into conflict with Lenin's government (though he left Russia before the Czech Legions began to fight against Bolshevik troops; was himself a strong opponent of large-scale Western intervention in the Russian civil war; and strongly advised President Woodrow Wilson against it). For the Soviet rulers, these few months are all that matter in Masaryk's life; he was an enemy of the Soviet Union, and had to be made an historical unperson. In the early 1950s the history of Czechoslovakia was systematically falsified along these lines. In the mid-1960s, under the relatively liberal rule of the last years of the Czech Communist Party boss Antonín Novotny, Czech historians began again to write the truth, and some excellent works appeared, from a socialist or a Marxist viewpoint of course, but good solid history. After 1968 orders were given for refalsification. Masaryk was to be an unperson again, and for good measure almost all prominent Czech historians were dismissed from their jobs. Those who were lucky were able to get jobs as unskilled workers, those who were not were thrown on the charity of relatives or friends. To be deprived of one's national history, to see one's national identity threatened, is something which Americans or West Europeans can hardly imagine happening to them. Historians should not, of course, overrate their own importance, but from some experience I am fairly sure of one thing: in the Danube countries, national history, or if you like historical mythology, is something about which not only professors of history but also working men and women, in factories and farms, feel bitterly. Attacks on it create a smouldering resentment which does not die out and can easily turn into a flame.

So we are faced with the determination on the one hand to humiliate whole nations and deprive them of their national identity, and on the other hand to preserve national identity in the face of outwardly overwhelming might. We have an irresistible force and an immovable object, or we might perhaps say an irrepressible conflict—one of those conflicts which are not solved by an apparently decisive victory, but reappear, perhaps in disguise or in genuinely modified form, like the ones which were not ended at Appomattox or at Potsdam, by the partition of India or the creation of Bangladesh, by the triumph of Pizarro over the Incas, or of the federal Nigerians over Biafra.

With the historian's professional deformation, I cannot help thinking of the analogy with Europe after

1815. Then order was established by great big imperial machines over rebellious troublemakers infected with liberal and nationalist heresies. Metternich and Tsar Nicholas seemed all-powerful. Yet their victorious regimes did not last.

They were not destroyed by *bourgeois* revolutions. There were of course revolutions, made as often by radical soldiers as by *bourgeois*, but to some extent by both—in Spain, in Naples, in Piedmont, in Poland, in Lombardy, in Austria, in Rome, in Bohemia, in Hungary, in Wallachia. All were crushed (the two apparent exceptions, Belgium and Greece, are not really exceptions because here Great Power diplomacy and armed force intervened). What overthrew the regime of Metternich and Nicholas, what got the ice melting, what opened the way for the forces of liberalism and capitalism and nationality to transform Europe, for better or worse, was not *bourgeois* revolution but war—in the Crimea, in Lombardy, in Moravia, and in Lorraine.

Now since 1945 too we have seen the triumph over the middle of Europe of a great big imperial machine, just one, and not three this time. And in less than thirty years there have been revolutions or revolts again, not *bourgeois* or proletarian (though the proletariat has been rather fully involved), but triggered off by very much the same sort of people, from the thinking classes, the intelligentsia, as in 1848. There have been risings in Pilzen and Berlin and Poznan and Warsaw, and all over Hungary and Bohemia and Moravia, and in Gdansk and Szczecin; and all have been crushed. But the difference between now and a hundred years ago is that the solution of that time—war

71

—cannot be used; or if it does come to that, it will destroy us all.

So should we conclude that the new empire has come to stay forever? Its leaders, insofar as they take seriously their much-trumpeted view of themselves as the infallible interpreters of exact Marxist-Leninist science, which explains the whole past, present, and future of human society, perhaps believe so. Hitler believed that he had founded the thousand-year Reich. The Soviet leaders operate at an intellectual level to which ordinary mortals cannot, or certainly should not aspire. All that I can say is that historical experience suggests that in the post-Enlightenment and post-industrial era empires do not last very long. This century has seen quite a few out. Palacký's last statement about the Habsburg Monarchy—"Before Austria was, we [the Czechs] existed, and after Austria is gone we shall still be there"—was realized earlier than he expected. Other empires too today are "one with Nineveh and Tyre." There is no Kipling writing in Russian, to warn the Soviet leaders against "such boasting as the Gentiles use, or lesser breeds without the law." Or should we perhaps say that Solzhenitsyn, with his warning, is performing a similar role? I fear the Soviet leaders will not listen to him. Braggarts and bullies they seem likely to remain. But that their empire is exempt from the laws of decay, decline, and fall, I gravely doubt.

It remains true that there is as yet little trace on the Soviet scene of a phenomenon that has long been prominent in the political class of Western nations, on both sides of the ocean—the imperial bad conscience, the collective guilt complex, the fear of being thought aggressive if one defends one's interest, the political loss of nerve. The Soviet leaders still seem to be firmly stuck in the age of Joseph Chamberlain and Theodore Roosevelt, with perhaps this difference—they carry a big stick but they don't bother to walk softly. Judging by the experience of other societies, the failure of nerve may come in the end, and there is certainly plenty to be guilty about. But what Lenin might have called a law of uneven development seems to be working to their advantage. There is a nerve-failure gap between West and East, which many enable the Soviet Union, despite its vulnerability to bureaucratic sclerosis, despite its tendency to fall ever more behind the West in economic and technical progress, nevertheless not only not to fall behind in relative military power or in will to dominate, but to gain relative strength, and to extend the geographical limits of its power. Against this there is the possibility that, just as the Balkan peoples escaped from Ottoman rule mainly because of the rise of a new Great Power in the East (at that time Russia), so the peoples of the heart of Europe may escape from their present masters by the rise of a Great Power that lies a great deal farther East. This has been for some years a subject of speculation among the Poles, although this does not of course prove that there is any sense in it.

These are gloomy speculations. It would be far pleasanter to believe that the voice of sweet reason, expressed with brilliant clarity and courage by academician Sakharov, many find listeners in high places; that it may be admitted that the doctrinaire arguments about "socialism" and "capitalism" are irrelevant in the face of the need of all great nations to cooperate in facing the terrible problems of world poverty, over-population, and pollution which threaten the whole human race. I wish that I could see signs that this was happening.

In conclusion I must return to the theme of Europe, which was the starting point and the very essence of what I have had to say. To identify the European Economic Community with "Europe" is absurd. If a Yorkshire businessman thinks his business will do better with Britain in the EEC, good luck to him, but Europe is more than that. If Frenchmen think that the EEC is France writ large, that it is just another episode in the long story of *Gesta Dei per Francos,* good luck to them too. I started my own formal education in a French school, and the passion of the French for their language and their culture is something that I, though an Anglo-Saxon barbarian, can partly share. But Europe is more than that. If Germans long to see their nation reunited, not along the old way which is now barred off, but in some new ways yet to be devised, good luck to them too. But Europe is more than that.

Today about eighty million Europeans are subjected to national humiliation, and this makes Europe one of the most explosive parts of the world. It is within the power of the Soviet leaders to put an end to national humiliation, and to content themselves with mere domination. This the peoples of the Danube lands would gladly accept. However, the choice lies only with the Soviet leaders. Sometimes Western journalists and politicians speak as if it lay within the power of the United States to ensure to the Soviets tranquility in the Danube lands, as if they could grant or withhold some magic recognition of the status quo which would relieve Muscovite minds of fear. But the truth is that this is not within the power of the United States, and would not be even if George Washington or Abraham Lincoln were at the helm. The remedy for the tension in the middle of Europe lies in Soviet hands alone. Only they can defuse the time bombs which they have been busily piling up.

Russia is in a sense a European power, but it also reaches far beyond Europe. The United States, and Canada too, are extra-European powers yet they too are in a sense European. Is Sverdlovsk or Tashkent more European than Minneapolis or Montreal?

The Soviet leaders can, if they wish, adopt the posture of the United States or Canada—let the Europeans be Europeans, while remaining on guard over their own interests in Europe, by whatever diplomatic or other means are required. Europe (not just the EEC) might in the long term form a constituent element in a world balance of five or six powers, but that is not even remotely in sight today.

The alternative for the Soviet leaders is to aim relentlessly at the capture of all Europe. Instead of lifting the nations of the Danube lands up to the level of Finland, they would first bring Western Europe down to the level of Finland, and then engulf them all. That way lies disaster. Meanwhile we are faced with uncertainty, unbending imperial arrogance, and wide-spread loss of nerve. I end by returning to my original metaphor. Europe remains the heart of the human race, and the heart of Europe is sick. The sickness will not be cured by pretending that it does not exist.